Family First Publishing Group

Revised First Edition

Canadian Cataloguing in Publication Data

Clerx, Sterling & Alexia
My Canadian Mom
www.mycanadianmom.ca

ISBN 978-1467923392

MY CANADIAN MOM

Story by Sterling and Alexia Clerx
Inspired by Shell Clerx (mom)
Edited by Gerald Clerx (dad)

Family **F**irst **P**ublishing **G**roup
Real Canadian stories inspired by real Canadian families ©

My Canadian mom loves spring when everything's fresh and new,
when flower blossoms and spider webs shimmer in morning dew.

She'll open all the windows up and remind us throughout the day,
to "breathe in all the fresh air," just like her mother used to say.

She'll put baskets on the patio
and flowers in every room,

for her springtime is a season
that couldn't have come too soon.

On Saturday's she encourages us both to sleep in till late,

then the three of us make breakfast as we plan our family date.

On Sundays we go hiking
along our favorite coastal trails,

watch bald eagles soar above us
and beside us orca whales.

My Canadian mom loves summer
        which starts on Canada Day,
at the parade we wave our flags
        and cheer "hip hip hooray."

We play outside, hop on our bikes and ride
        down to our favourite park,
we run and hide, skim down our 'slip and slide'
        and roast marshmallows after dark.

Mom loves to take us camping ... we stay up late into the night, watching shooting stars streak across the dancing Northern lights.

We listen to the silence ... the stillness in the air,
when the sounds of Mother Nature is all that you can hear.

My Canadian mom loves autumn, when the leaves turn fiery red,
telling us that snowfall is just a few more weeks ahead.

She loves for us to play outdoors and when it starts to rain,
she calls us in ... she warms us up ... then sends us out again.

Mom loves to stroll down country lanes lined with maple trees,
walking hand in hand with us, kicking up the leaves.

She talks to us so lovingly about this world that we all live in,
that we should be so thankful for this gift that we've been given.

My Canadian mom is happiest
        when the family all stays home,
it seems she has a thing about us
        not feeling left alone.

We've watched the Sound of Music
        at least a dozen times,
she's memorized the songs they sing
        and almost all their lines.

My Canadian mom loves winter
she was raised in prairie snow,
and doesn't bat a frozen eyelash
even when it's 30 below.

She's game for any weather
it doesn't matter if it's bleak,
she can make a toque and matching mittens
look really, really chic.

She loves it when the snow falls
blanketing everything in white,
the moonlit glow on fresh fallen snow
is her very favourite sight.

And when the snow gets really deep
it never ever fails,
she'll go and get the snowshoes out
and take us hiking through the trails.

My Canadian mom is always helping out
        especially those in need,
when it comes to pitching in
        she'll always take the lead.

Mom was brought up on the prairies
        where helping out is what you do,
She tells us "when you give to others
        it always comes back to you."

Mom behaves in very humble ways
        she's modest to the core,
when it comes to who's got more of what
        she doesn't bother keeping score.

My Canadian mom's no techie
    she thinks an Apple is a fruit,
her friends can tweet and google
    but she doesn't give a hoot.

She's tried out all this high tech stuff
    but prefers the "good old days,"
when tweeting was something birds would do
    and chatting was face to face.

Mom doesn't read the papers
    or watch the evening news cast,
she'd rather be living in the present
    than worrying about the past.

My Canadian mom loves this country ... she tells us every day,
   "after God created Canada, the mold was thrown away."

It's flanked by rugged coastlines and forests of ever green,
   it has endless seas of golden wheat filling up the in between.

It's home to polar bears and grizzly bears, black and Kodiak too,
   harp seals, wolves and 9 foot moose, just to name a few.

My Canadian mom encourages us
     to be the best that we can be,
and says there's no greater blessing
     than the gift of family.

She is always standing by our side
     no matter what we do,
and when she tucks us in at night
     mom tells us …

"I love you."

About OUR Canadian Mom

 This story was inspired by our Canadian mom Shell. She was born in Winnipeg, Manitoba and spent her childhood in the prairies. Her favorite memories growing up were playing kick the can with her neighborhood friends and spending time with her Ukranian "Bubba" making perogies and cabbage rolls. She has always loved the simple things in life like big family gatherings, evening walks and family games nights.

We think you will love reading about our Canadian mom. She's a very unique woman who stands up for what she believes in ... even if she ruffles a few feathers along the way.

What about YOUR Canadian Mom

Do you know of a Canadian mom with a story worth sharing? If so, tell us and we'll help you share her story in our "My Canadian Mom" children's book series. To learn more go to our website at www.mycanadianmom.ca.